THE NEGOTIATOR'S COOK BOOK
LEABHAR CÓCAIREACHTA AN IDIRBHEARTAITHE

Le Gerry Adams
Agus le giota beag cuidithe ó
Ted Howell agus Pádraic Wilson

Gerry Adams
with a little help from
Ted Howell and Pádraic Wilson

THE NEGOTIATORS COOK BOOK – BEST KEPT SECRET OF THE IRISH PEACE PROCESS

Pádraic being dragged away from his stove

Gerry waiting for him in Room 316

Thanks

My thanks to Ted, Pádraic, Michelle, Iseult, Maura and Caral for their recipes. To Rosemary for the typing. RG for technical advice. Many thanks to Séamus, Neil and Johnny for translations. Mark for design and Desi for his incisive ridicule.

Buíochas

Gabhaim mo bhuíochas le Ted, Pádraic, Michelle, Maura, Iseult agus Carál as a gcuid oideas a roinnt liom; agus le Rosemary as an chlóscríbhneoireacht. Míle buíochas le Séamus, Neil agus Johnny mar gheall ar an Ghaeilge. Tá mé an-bhuíoch fosta de Mark as an dearadh, agus de Desi as an mhagadh ghéarchúiseach.

This book is dedicated to the memory of Siobhán O'Hanlon, to Sinn Féin's Negotiating Team and to cooks everywhere.

Tá an leabhar seo tiomnaithe i gcuimhne Siobhán O'Hanlon, do Fhoireann Idirbheartaíochta Shinn Féin agus do chócairí ar fud an bhaill.

My first negotiation was in June, 1972. I was released from internment in Long Kesh to join Dáithí Ó Conaill in a meeting with senior British officials and Belfast lawyer PJ McGrory. Our talks led to a bi-lateral truce between the IRA and the British forces and another meeting in London between republicans and the British Government. The truce collapsed soon after and the conflict resumed. There were other failed efforts to negotiate an end to hostilities. That's a lot of negotiations. It was forty years before they were successful.

The first negotiation I was involved in were very straight forward. Perhaps both sides were naive. Maybe that's why they failed. Since then I've learned that negotiating a change in British Government policy in Ireland, and its consequences, is a complicated business. Especially when the issues involved are as deep rooted and fundamental as those which have underpinned conflict and division in Ireland for a very long time. Such an endeavour needs people with special skills. With stamina and persistence, patience and clear objectives. To be successful means being very focussed and united with an eye for detail and an informed knowledge of the issues they are dealing with.

• Sinn Féin Ard Chomhairle meeting in 44 Parnell Square

The in the-room-negotiators, usually the leaders and senior advisers, rarely have all this detail themselves. So other comrades with that expertise are drafted in to support them. Over the years Sinn Féin developed a remarkable group of people to fulfil these responsibilities. Uniquely they also, or the main core of comrades involved, remained the same for almost forty years.

• Sinn Féin meeting
in Stormont

But we weren't on our own. We also had very clear lines of communication with, and guidance or direction, from the leadership not directly involved in the talks. In Sinn Féin's case this involves our national leadership - An Ard Chomhairle. Most other parties operate a similar system of report back.

This includes the two governments. Of course, the British and Irish governments have huge resources in comparison to the political parties and the British government has a long history of negotiations and all the skills, and a tendency for duplicity and skulduggery that comes with this record.

A history of negotiations from the Irish republican perspective deserves a book all on its own. This is not that book.

This is a cook book. A Negotiators Cook Book. Why so? Because when a negotiations team assembles, sometimes for days, occasionally for weeks, they need to be fed.

• Delegation on way to first
meeting at Downing Street

Tony Blair and Jonathan Powell, the Chief of Staff of his office used to joke that I always raised the issue of food with them if and when we met in London for protracted talks.

"And why not?" I would protest. *"Surely if people are going to work for long periods food should be provided on site. Otherwise the dynamics of a process can be undermined if those involved - and this may assist the maligners - have to leave for nourishment. That's why chuck wagons were invented".*

Martin McGuinness, an outstanding Chuck, was usually bemused by my pleas.

But Downing Street has no capacity or desire for such necessities. At times if talks stretched beyond meal times Pizzas or Chinese takeaways would be summoned. I often wondered what the purveyors in the take

• On way into 10 Downing Street, London

away joint thought when they got the phone call for multi servings of Sweet and Sour, Noodles or Pepperoni for delivery to Downing Street.

Surely I said to Mr Blair would it not be better to plan for proper food when his officials were organizing long sessions. Even to keep folks in good form.

And I was not the only one to note this shortcoming. Brian Faulkner in his book *'Brian Faulkner – Memoirs Of A Statesman'*, published in 1978 after his death, writes about a crisis meeting in Downing Street on 19 August 1969 between the leaders of the old unionist Government, Major Chichester Clark. Robert Porter and himself, with British PM Harold Wilson, James Callaghan and others.

Mr Faulkner complains that there was no food provided.

> *'The whole meeting lasted from 2pm to 11pm, and the standard of Downing Street hospitality was not up to scratch on this occasion; Harold said there was no food available. The Northern Ireland representatives' last meal had been breakfast that morning. I was very grateful to Denis Healey, the decent man who shared his sandwiches with me.'*

It's little wonder the old regime wasted away.

In our time tea was always served on arrival at Number 10. A friendly wee woman from Monaghan was the main person on tea duty. She was very conscious of the meagre fare offered "especially after our journey from home". It was what my Granny used to call an Englishman's cup of

• With Albert Reynolds and John Hume

THE NEGOTIATORS COOK BOOK – BEST KEPT SECRET OF THE IRISH PEACE PROCESS

Locked Out Of Talks. 10 June 1996

tea. That is tea on its own. Or coffee. My Granny never handed a cup of tea like that to anyone. Our Monaghan friend would know it was always accompanied by cake, or buns or more usually homemade soda or wheaten bread and butter. Martin McGuinness's mother Peggy was the same.

Sometimes the farls were warm from the griddle with the butter melting on it and dribbling down your chin. Ma Hamill did the same for young scholars from my old school Saint Mary's. According to Ted, Ma Hamill's shop was raided sometimes by 'The Boss' - Brother Murphy to wreck Seamie Drumm's card school in the back room. Ach sin scéal eile. Ma Hamill dispatched warm bread smothered in jam or butter from her wee shop in Divis Street below An Ard Scoil in Belfast, to young card sharps and ordinary decent Saint Mary's students. She even had soda farls with currants in them. A rare treat.

Unfortunately there was no Ma Hamill in Number 10.

I told them once, that we Irish have an ancestral hunger. Some of us also understand the social importance and mutual relationship building benefits of breaking bread together.

For their part the Irish government always provided good grub on the big occasions that they hosted lengthy talks sessions. I thought this showed the cultural differences between the two sides. Brian Faulkner would have approved.

• Martin McGuinness, Pat Doherty, Lucilita Breathnach, Martin Ferris and Rita O Hare at The Forum for Peace and Reconciliation In Dublin

THE NEGOTIATORS COOK BOOK – BEST KEPT SECRET OF THE IRISH PEACE PROCESS

One time, Ian Paisley was to meet the Taoiseach in London for a morning get together. In the Irish Embassy. As this was his first time to visit the Embassy there was much media attention. Later Mr Paisley reported that when asked in advance what he wanted for breakfast he ordered boiled eggs.

"I knew they couldn't interfere with those" he joked.

He quite rightly took it as a given that breakfast would be provided. That's what you do when you are a gracious host. Or a gracious guest.

• Part of the Sinn Féin Negotiating team in Stormont

The chef at the Embassy is a star. He once provided, at my request a very nice batch of sandwiches for Ray, our London driver of Crossmaglen roots, to eat on the way back to the airport. It's hard to match the London Irish.

Some set piece events in England featured decent dinners and on other private occasions Tony Blair would treat Martin and I to whatever was on the menu, particularly at Chequers which he used a lot at weekends.

When Tony Blair left office and Gordon Brown followed him it became clear that if New Labour had a marked inability to provide vittles as part of routine logistics the Tories were even worse, probably for ideological reasons. That was definitely a cultural deficiency. An Upstairs Downstairs mentality.

Later when the power sharing government was established most of the talks were held in Ireland, usually in Belfast at Stormont. That's when Ted Howell came into his own. His culinary contributions to the Republican peace processers mark the time we spent at Stormont either in Room 316 or in Martin

• Room 316 in Stormont

McGuinness's office in Stormont Castle. Ted would arrive with buckets of good healthy nourishing soup and cakes of home baked bread. That's how it all began.

Later he went on to add pasta dishes, salads, home cooked hams, pies of all shapes and sizes, fish dishes or veggie meals for RG our resident token wannibee veggie and other meals of choice for those comrades with allergies or other eating tendencies. Incidentally, RG is actually a Pescatarian, a Free Pescatarian. He eats fish and sea food but not the flesh of other animals.

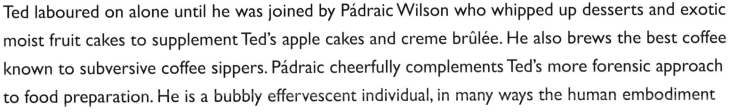

The Vegetarian Society has made it clear that eating fish is not a vegetarian diet. I offer that up as proof that nothing is ever simple. There is a split in everything. As Leonard might say *"That's how the light gets in."*

Ted laboured on alone until he was joined by Pádraic Wilson who whipped up desserts and exotic moist fruit cakes to supplement Ted's apple cakes and creme brûlée. He also brews the best coffee known to subversive coffee sippers. Pádraic cheerfully complements Ted's more forensic approach to food preparation. He is a bubbly effervescent individual, in many ways the human embodiment of his delightful sweet creations. Between them, and their generous giving natures, Ted and Pádraic are the perfect cooking couple. Pádraic, unlike Ted, is also good at food shopping. And, unlike Ted, he has a car which is useful when transporting meals for more than a dozen comrades.

This book is a memorial to their cooking skills,

• After St Andrews Agreement, Scotland

kindness, cordon bleu ideals and tenacity. Both these catering Colossuses are veteran Republican activists with chequered stories in the wider narrative of resistance to British rule in Ireland, the peace process and the search for justice and equality. But that is a story they must tell themselves. Or not tell if that is their desire. Suffice to say their valued involvement in the negotiations process was not limited to their catering contributions. But it is a memorable aspect of it. Not least because the likes of Gerry Kelly put on weight during some of the more strenuous episodes of talks. So did Martin McGuinness.

The fare Ted and Pádraic rustled up for our team, and occasionally a wayward Unionist or Irish Government Minister or their staff, and the recipes involved, are not limited to those who cook for peace processes. These dishes would grace any dinner table. They are ideal for pre-packed lunches or picnics. Easily transported and where appropriate reheat-able without too much fuss.

They are also healthy and nourishing. Except for Pádraic's sugary creations. But they did give us a boost when we were flagging during marathon sessions. Comfort food for the soul. I commend them to you. Ted and Pádraic are the stars of this epistle. They helped to sustain the peace process.

• Martin and Jim Gibney

• After the Hillsborough Peace Talks 2003

THE NEGOTIATORS COOK BOOK – BEST KEPT SECRET OF THE IRISH PEACE PROCESS

Ba i mí an Mheithimh 1972 an chéad idirbheartaíocht ina raibh mé páirteach. Scaoileadh saor mé ón Cheis Fhada, mar a raibh mé imtheorannaithe, chun dul in éineacht le Dáithí Ó Conaill chuig cruinniú le hoifigigh shinsearacha de chuid na Breataine agus an dlíodóir ó Bhéal Feirste PJ McGrory. De bharr na gcainteanna siúd, tháinig sos cogaidh ar an fhód idir Óglaigh na hÉireann agus fórsaí na Breataine; agus bhí cruinniú eile ann idir phoblachtaigh agus Rialtas na Breataine. Thit an sos cogaidh as a chéile go gairid ina dhiaidh sin agus thosaigh an choinbhleacht arís féin. Bhí iarrachtaí eile ann chun deireadh na cogaíochta a shocrú tríd an idirbheartaíocht; ach theip orthu. Sin cuid mhór idirbheartaíochta. Chuaigh daichead bliain thart sula raibh rath orthu.

Na chéad chainteanna idirbheartaíochta a raibh baint agamsa leo, bhí siad simplí go leor. B'fhéidir go raibh an dá thaobh soineanta. B'fhéidir gur sin an fáth ar theip orthu. Ó shin i leith, tá sé foghlamtha agam gur gnoithe casta é polasaí Rialtas na Breataine maidir le hÉirinn, agus a impleachtaí, gur casta an rud é sin a athrú trí idirbheartaíocht. Go háirithe, nuair atá na hábhair fréamhaithe chomh domhain sin agus nuair atá siad chomh buntábhachtach sin gur chothaigh siad coinbhleacht agus deighilt in Éirinn leis na blianta fada. Le hiarrachtaí mar seo, bíonn daoine de dhíth a bhfuil scileanna speisialta acu. Fuinneamh agus dianseasmhacht, foighne agus cuspóirí soiléire. Le go mbeadh rath ar na hiarrachtaí sin, caithfear bheith ar aon intinn agus aire a choimheád ar an chúram agus ar na mionsonraí; ní foláir bheith ar an eolas faoi na hábhair a bhfuil siad ag plé leo.

Is annamh a bhíonn an t-eolas mionsonraithe sin ar fad ag na hidirbheartaithe a théann sa tseomra; na ceannairí nó na comhairleoirí sinsearacha, de ghnáth. Tugtar comrádaithe eile isteach chun tacaíocht a thabhairt dóibh. Le linn na mblianta, forbraíodh grúpa den scoth de

dhaoine in Sinn Féin leis na freagrachtaí sin a chur i gcrích. Go speisialta, d'fhan an grúpa seo, nó an chuid is mó den ghrúpa, d'fhan sé mar a gcéanna ar feadh beagnach daichead bliain.

Ach ní raibh muid linn féin. Bhí bealaí soiléire cumarsáide againn, le haghaidh comhairle nó treorach, leis na ceannairí nach raibh baint dhíreach acu leis na cainteanna. I gcás Shinn Féin, baineann sé seo lenár struchtúr náisiúnta ceannaireachta – An Ard Chomhairle. Tá córas den chineál sin ag an chuid is mó de na páirtithe eile.

Bíodh an dá rialtas san áireamh. Ar ndóigh, ní beag na hacmhainní atá ag Rialtas na Breataine agus an Rialtas in Éireann i gcomparáid leis na páirtithe polaitiúla; agus tá stair fhada ag Rialtas na Breataine maidir le hidirbheartaíocht agus na scileanna, agus calaois a théann léi.

B'fhiú leabhar a dhíriú ar stair na n-idirbheartaíochtaí ón dearcadh phoblachtach féin. Ní hé seo an leabhar sin.

Is leabhar cócaireachta é seo. Leabhar Cócaireachta an Idirbheartaithe. Cad chuige sin? Nuair a thagann foireann idirbheartaíochta le chéile, uaireanta go ceann cúpla lá, amanna go ceann seachtainí, caithfear iad a chothú.

Bhíodh Tony Blair agus Jonathon Powell, Ceann Foirne a oifige, ag magadh go dtógainn ceist an bhia i gcónaí nuair a bhímis in Londain do chainteanna a mhaireadh tamall fada.

"Agus cad chuige nach dtógfainn?" a déarfainn mar argóint. "Leoga, más rud é go mbeidh daoine ag obair ar feadh na n-uaireanta fada, ba chóir go mbeadh bia ar fáil ar an láthair. Sin nó bainfear an bonn ón phróiseas,

más gá dóibh siúd atá páirteach imeacht le hiad féin a chothú – rud a chuideodh leis na scriostóirí, b'fhéidir. Sin ba chúis le ceapadh na Chuck Wagons."

Bhíodh Martin McGuinness, Chuck den chéad scoth, trí chéile agam agus mé ag impí orthu bia a sholáthar. Ach níl an cumas iontu ná an mhian ar lucht Downing Street i leith na riachtanas siúd. Uaireanta má mhair na cainteanna thar am béile, chuirtí fios ar na Pizzas nó ar an Bhialann beir-leat Síneach. Ba mhinic a dhéanainn mo mhachnamh ar na ceannaithe-beir-leat agus ar cad é a shíleadh siad nuair a fuair siad glao gutháin ag iarraidh orthu riaranna den bhéile milis searbh, nuadail nó piobarónaí a chur chuig Downing Street.

Dúirt mé le Blair, go mbeadh sé i bhfad níb fhearr bia ceart a sholáthar nuair a bhíodh a chuid oifigeach ag eagrú na seisiún fada. Go fiú leis an dea-fhonn a choinneáil ar dhaoine.

Ní mise amháin a thug an t-easnamh sin faoi deara. Ina leabhar a foilsíodh i ndiaidh a bháis 'Brian Faulkner – Memoirs of a Statesman', scríobhann Brian Faulkner faoi chruinniú géarchéime in Downing Street ar 19 Lúnasa 1969 idir ceannairí an tseanrialtais aontachtaigh Major Chichester Clark, Robert Porter, Faulkner é féin, agus Príomhaire na Breataine Harold Wilson, James Callaghan agus eile.

Déanann Faulkner a ghearán nár cuireadh bia ar bith ar fáil.

"Mhair an cruinniú ar fad ón 2in go dtí 11in, agus ní raibh an fháilte sásúil go leor ar an ócáid seo; dúirt Harold nach raibh aon bhia ar fáil. Ba é bricfeasta na maidine sin an béile deireanach a bhí ag ionadaithe Thuaisceart Éireann. Bhí mé

iontach buíoch de Denis Healey, an fear uasal a roinn a chuid ceapairí liom."

Ní hiontas gur imigh an seanréimeas as.

Lenár linn féin, chuirtí an tae ar an tábla ar theacht isteach go Downing Street dúinn. Bean bheag chairdiúil as Muineachán a bhí i mbun na ndualgas tae go príomha. Bhí a fhios aici go maith gur tearc an féasta, go háirithe "i ndiaidh ár dturais ón bhaile". Ba é an rud ar a dtugadh mo mháthair mhór - cupán tae Sasanaigh. Sin tae leis féin. Nó caife. Cupán tae mar sin níor thug mo mháthair mhór riamh do dhuine ná deoraí. Bheadh a fhios ag bean Mhuineacháin gur le císte, nó bonnóga ba chóir a thabhairt, nó níos minice ná a mhalairt, le harán sóide nó cruithneachta agus im. Mar a chéile do Peggy, máthair Martin McGuinness.

Uaireanta, bhí na farlanna te ón ghrideall agus an t-im ag leá orthu, agus é ag sileadh síos an smig agat. Rinne Ma Hamill amhlaidh do na scoláirí óga ó Naomh Muire. Dar le Ted, dhéanadh The Boss – an Bráthair Murphy - ruathar ar shiopa Ma Hamill ó am go chéile le scoil cártaí Seamie Drumm, a bhíodh sa tseomra cúil, le hí sin a scriosadh. Ach sin scéal eile. Sheoladh Ma Hamill arán te clúdaithe le subh nó im, sheoladh sí sin óna siopa beag i Sráid Duibhis taobh thíos den Ard Scoil i mBéal Feirste, chuig na cúigleálaithe óga agus

chuig na gnáthscoláirí macánta in Naomh Muire. Fiú amháin, bhí farlanna sóide ina raibh cuiríní aici. Ba phléisiúr annamh sin.

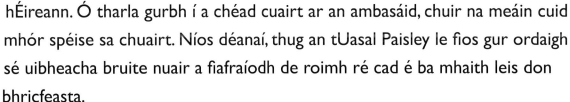

Ar an drochuair, ní raibh a leithéid de Ma Hamill le fáil in Uimhir 10.

Dúirt mé leo uair amháin go bhfuil ocras sinseartha orainne mar Éireannaigh. Tuigeann cuid againn, fosta, an tábhacht sóisialta agus na buntáistí maidir le caidrimh comhthuisceana a fhorbairt, tuigeann cuid againn mar a bhaineann sé sin le béile a chaitheamh le chéile.

Ó thaobh Rialtas na hÉireann de, chuireadh siadsan togha na beatha ar fáil i gcónaí ar na hócáidí móra nuair a reáchtáil siad cainteanna fada. Cheap mé féin gur léirigh sé sin an difear idir an dá thaobh. Bheadh Brian Faulkner sásta leis sin.

Maidin amháin, bhí Ian Paisley chun bualadh leis an Taoiseach i Londain. In Ambasáid na hÉireann. Ó tharla gurbh í a chéad cuairt ar an ambasáid, chuir na meáin cuid mhór spéise sa chuairt. Níos déanaí, thug an tUasal Paisley le fios gur ordaigh sé uibheacha bruite nuair a fiafraíodh de roimh ré cad é ba mhaith leis don bhricfeasta.

"Bhí a fhios agam nach dtiocfadh leo cur isteach orthu sin," ar seisean ag magadh.

Ghlac sé leis, mar ba chóir, go gcuirfear bricfeasta ar fáil. Sin an rud a dhéanann tú mar óstach flaithiúil. Nó mar chuairteoir flaithiúil.

Bhí an cócaire san Ambasáid thar barr. Uair den tsaol, ar m'iarratas féin, sholáthair

sé pacáiste ceapairí do Ray, ár dtiománaí Londanach ar de phór Chrois Mhic Lionnáin é le go mbeadh greim aige ar an bhealach ar ais chuig an aerfort. Is doiligh Éireannaigh Londan a shárú.

Bhí dinnéar maith ar fáil ag cuid de na hócáidí móra i Sasana agus ar ócáidí eile príobháideacha nuair a chuir Tony Blair cá bith rud a bhí ar an chlár bia os ár gcomhair, go háirithe ag Chequers mar a gcaitheadh sé go leor deireadh seachtaine.

Nuair a d'éirigh Tony Blair as oifig agus tháinig Gordon Blair ina dhiaidh, b'fhollasach dúinn mura raibh cumas ar bith ag New Labour soláthairtí a chur ar fáil, gur mheasa arís a bhí na Tóraithe, ar chúiseanna idé-eolaíocha is dócha. Ba easnamh cultúrtha sin go cinnte. Meon a bhaineann leis an deighilt idir uasal agus íseal.

Ina dhiaidh sin nuair a bunaíodh an rialtas comhroinnte cumhachta, reáchtáladh an chuid is mó de na cainteanna in Éirinn, ag Cnoc an Anfa i mBéal Feirste go hiondúil. Sin an t-am ar tháinig Ted Howell i dtreis. D'fhág a chuid cócaireachta a rian ar an lucht próisis síochána, ag marcáil an ama a gcaití i Seomra 316 nó in oifig Martin McGuinness i gCaisleán Chnoc an Anfa. Thagadh Ted le buicéid de shú sláintiúil folláin agus cistí d'arán bácáilte baile. Agus sin mar a thosaigh sé ar fad.

Ina dhiaidh sin, thug sé béilí pasta, sailéid, liamháis cócaráilte sa bhaile, pióga de gach cineál, éisc nó béile veigeatóireach do RG, ár wannabe veigeatóir

comharthach, agus rogha na mbéilí eile do na comrádaithe siúd a bhfuil ailléirge orthu nó claonta ithe eile acu. Mar a tharlaíonn, is pescatarian RG le fírinne. Itheann sé éisc agus bia mara, ach ní itheann feoil ainmhithe eile. Tá sé curtha in iúl ag The Vegetarian Society nach ionann éisc a ithe agus aiste bia an veigeatóra. Molaim sin mar fhianaise nach mbíonn rud ar bith simplí riamh. Bíonn scoilt ann i gcónaí. Mar a deir Leonard, "sin mar a thagann an solas isteach".

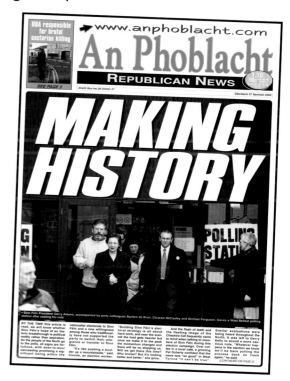

Chaith Ted an dua ina aonar gur tháinig Pádraic Wilson. Chruthaíodh Pádraic milseoga agus cístí boga coimhthíocha torthaí chun cur leis na cácaí úll agus crepe Brûlée a rinne Ted. Chomh maith leis sin, déanann sé an caife is fearr dá bhfuil ar eolas ag óltóirí ceannairceacha caife. Cuireann Pádraic go croíúil leis an chur chuige níos fóiréinsí atá ag Ted. Is duine bríomhar gealgháireach é; agus ar a lán dóigheanna, is léiriú i gcorp daonna é ar a chuid cruthúchán siúcraithe. Idir an bheirt acu, agus a meon fial flaithiúil, is lánúin fhoirfe cócaireachta iad. Murab ionann agus Ted, tá Pádraic go maith fosta ag an tsiopadóireacht bia. Agus, murab ionann agus Ted, tá carr aige; rud atá úsáideach chun béilí a iompar le haghaidh níos mó ná dosaen comrádaithe.

Is in ómós dá scileanna cócaireachta, dá gcineáltas, dá gcuid idéal cordon bleu agus in ómós dá ndiongbháilteacht atá an leabhar seo. Is seanfhondúirí den streachailt phoblachtach beirt fhathach seo na cócaireachta. Tá stair chorach acu beirt ag cur in aghaidh riail na Breataine in Éirinn, sa phróiseas síochána agus sa troid ar son córa agus comhionannais. Ach is scéal é sin nach mór dóibh féin a insint. Nó gan é a insint más sin a mian. Is leor a rá nár bhain fiúntas a gcuid oibre sa phróiseas idirbheartaíochta leis an chócaireacht amháin. Is cuid speisialta dá gcuid iarrachtaí é, mar sin féin. Go háirithe nó chuir Gerry Kelly suas go leor meáchain le linn cuid de na tréimhsí diana cainteanna. B'amhlaidh do Martin McGuinness.

An bia a chuir Ted agus Pádraic ar fáil don fhoireann s'againn, agus corruair don aontachtóir ar strae nó d'Aire ó Rialtas na hÉireann nó dá mbaill foirne, an bia agus a gcuid oideas, níl siad teoranta dóibh siúd a dhéanann cócaireacht do phróisis síochána.

Bheadh siad in áit an ghrásta ar aon bhord dinnéir. Tá siad foirfe don lón réamhphacáilte nó don phicnic. Iniompartha go héasca agus nuair is cuí, intéite arís gan mórán stró.

Tá siad sláintiúil folláin freisin. Seachas cruthúcháin siúcraithe Phadraic. Ach neartaigh siad muid nuair a bhí muid ag dul i léig le linn na seisiún fada. Bia baile don anam. Molaim daoibh iad. Is iad Ted agus Pádraic laochra na heipistile seo. Chuidigh siad leis an phróiseas síochána a chothú.

Photo by pepperdream at Morguefile.com

CONTENTS | CLÁR

BREADS | ARÁN

I have known Ted for a very long time. He is very knowledgeable in his own right. In addition, he also has a finely honed ability to appear knowledgeable even on issues that he knows nothing about. But Ted does know about bread. He is also a compulsive baker. For my part, I have stopped eating bread, although I do eat cake. But that's another story. Ted told me once that that there are dozens of types of bread. But, he went on, the most commonly known to, and used by us, on Paddy's Green Shamrock Shore are those leavened by yeast or soda – bicarbonate of soda or baking soda.

Yeast breads – especially granary meal – used to be a Ted speciality. But it takes time. So Ted decided that baking them is for the retired or teetotallers. On the other hand soda bread can be prepared in about fifteen minutes. So it has been soda bread that Ted generally served to the Sinn Féin negotiating team. He divides those into four categories:

🍴 Fruit 🍴 Treacle 🍴 Wheaten 🍴 Brack

These are his recipes. On top of the fifteen minutes preparation they take about an hour to bake.

Photo by pickle at Morguefile.com

Tá aithne agam ar Ted le fada an lá. Tá sé an-eolach ar a dhóigh féin. Lena chois sin, tá an-slacht ar a chumas cuma an eolais a thabhairt air féin, fiú maidir le hábhair a bhfuil sé dall ar fad orthu. Tá sé feasach faoin arán, áfach. Ní stadann sé de bheith ag báicéireacht. Ó mo thaobhsa de, ní ithim arán níos mó, cé go n-ithim cístí. Ach sin scéal eile. Dúirt Ted liom uair den tsaol go bhfuil na scórtha de chineálacha aráin ann. Ach, lean sé leis, is iad sin atá laibhínithe trí ghiosta nó sóid - décharbónáit sóidiam nó sóid aráin – is iad sin na cinn is coitianta ar Chruacha Glasa na hÉireann

Bhíodh aráin déanta de ghiosta ina shainbhia ag Ted. Ach bíonn an t-am ag teastáil. Mar sin de, chinn Ted gur arán le haghaidh daoine atá ar scor iad sin; sin nó na staonairí. Ar an lámh eile, is féidir arán sóide a dhéanamh taobh istigh de chúig bhomaite dhéag. Dá réir sin, is é an t-arán sóide atá curtha ar fáil ag Ted d'fhoireann idirbheartaíochta Shinn Féin, den chuid is mó. Tá ceithre rangú in úsáid aige:

🍴 Toradh 🍴 Triacla 🍴 Cruithneachta 🍴 Bairín breac

Seo a leanas a chuid oideas. Chomh maith leis an chúig bhomaite dhéag chun iad a ullmhú, tógfaidh sé thart faoi uair an chloig le hiad a bhácáil.

Fruit Soda | Sóid Torthaí

Pre-heat the oven to 180° Fahrenheit.

🍴 *Sieve 1 1/2 lbs of plain flour, and 2 teaspoons each, of sugar, salt and baking powder into a bowl.*

🍴 *Add a good fistful of sultanas or dried fruit or raisins. Mix the dry ingredients.*

🍴 *Make a well in the flour/fruit mixture and add a pint of buttermilk or sweet milk. Preferably the former. Mix gently from the side of the bowl.*

🍴 *Turn into a well-greased 2lb loaf tin. Place in the centre of the oven and bake for 1 hour approximately.*

Turn out onto the kitchen top. Tap the bottom. If it sounds hollow then it's baked.
Wrap in a clean T-cloth and place on a wire rack to cool.

- 1 1/2 lbs of plain flour
- 2 teaspoons sugar
- 2 teaspoons salt
- 2 teaspoons baking powder
- Good fistful of sultanas or dried fruit or raisins
- 1 pint buttermilk or sweet milk

Treacle | Triacla

Same quantities of flour, salt, sugar, soda and milk. But add a half tin of treacle to the milk. Using a low heat on the hob to combine the milk/treacle. Mix as above and tip into a greased 2lb loaf tin. One hour to bake as above.

- 1 1/2 lbs of plain flour
- 2 teaspoons sugar
- 2 teaspoons salt
- 2 teaspoons baking powder
- Good fistful of sultanas or dried fruit or raisins
- 1 pint buttermilk or sweet milk
- 1/2 tin of treacle

Wheaten | Cruithneachta

Two pounds of dry ingredients and two pints of milk go into this.

🍴 *12 ozs coarse wholemeal flour*

🍴 *12 ozs porridge oats*

🍴 *8 ozs of any combination of pinhead oatmeal, bulgur wheat, oat bran, wheat bran or even cous cous. Or just one of them.*

🍴 *Two teaspoons each of salt, bicarbonate of soda.*

🍴 *Mix as above and tip into 3 well-greased 1lb loaf tins. Bake for 1 hour approximately. Test for cookedness and cooling as above.*

- 12 ozs coarse wholemeal flour
- 12 ozs porridge oats
- 8 ozs of any combination of pinhead oatmeal, bulgur wheat, oat bran, wheat bran or even cous cous
- 2 teaspoons salt
- 2 teaspoons bicarbonate of soda
- 2 pint buttermilk or sweet milk

THE NEGOTIATORS COOK BOOK – BEST KEPT SECRET OF THE IRISH PEACE PROCESS

Brack | Bairín breac

A humble first cousin of the more sophisticated Barmbrack which is leavened with yeast. Keeps much better than the other soda breads set out above.

As per usual, have your oven pre-heated to 180°Fahrenheit and a well-greased 2lb loaf tin.

- 1lb dried fruit (sultanas, raisins, mixed fruit or whatever you have)
- 2 teaspoons of baking soda
- 2 teaspoons of salt
- 1 pint of boiling water
- 1lb of flour
- 8 ozs of soft brown sugar
- 2 teaspoons of mixed spice or cinnamon

Put 1lb dried fruit (sultanas, raisins, mixed fruit: whatever you have); 2 teaspoons of baking soda and 2 of salt into a bowl.

Add a pint of boiling water and leave for 10-15 minutes to allow fruit to soften.

Add 1lb of flour, 8ozs of soft brown sugar and 2 teaspoons of mixed spice or cinnamon.

Mix well and tip into a 2lb tin.

Bake for 1 hour approximately and leave for 15 minutes or so before attempting to remove from tin.

Ted serves these breads with butter or jam or as a side dish to his fine salads or soups. He also makes a chickpea hummus type yoke or tuna and smoked mackerel paté type treats. Ted's bread plastered with these spreads is both tasty and nutritious.

SALADS | SAILÉID

⚟ Chickpea and Tuna ⚟ Smoked Mackerel ⚟ Potato ⚟ Celeriac ⚟ Beanz ⚟ Beetroot ⚟ Greens ⚟ Dressing

Ted is very strategic. I think he stumbled into those dishes while socially wandering in warmer climes. They suit our needs because re-heating facilities are limited to a microwave and cooking facilities are non-existent in Stormont Castle or Room 316 in Parliament Buildings. Salads are also popular with the generation of republican grazers that has sprung up since The Good Friday Agreement. But Ted believes that carnivores are an increasingly threatened species so he tries to satisfy all tastes. He adds cold cuts of meat. The variety of salads available is as infinite as his patience, generosity and capacity for good wine. In other words unlimited. But for this publication he has offered a handful. A seven fingered hand he tells me.

⚟Sicphiseánach agus Tuinnín ⚟Murlas Deataithe ⚟Prátaí ⚟Soiliriac ⚟Pónairí ⚟Biatas ⚟Glasraí glasa ⚟Blastán

Tá Ted iontach straitéiseach mar dhuine. Sílim gur tháinig sé ar na béilí sin de thaisme agus é ag spaisteoireacht i dtíortha níos teo. Oireann siad go maith dúinn nó tá na hacmhainní atéite teoranta don oigheann mhicreathonnach agus níl ann do na háiseanna cócaireachta i gCaisleán Chnoc an Anfa nó i Seomra 316 ag Foirgnimh na Parlaiminte. Tá an-tóir ar na sailéid ag iteoirí poblachtacha a tháinig chun cinn sa ré i ndiaidh Chomhaontú Aoine an Chéasta. Ach creideann Ted gur speicis atá i mbaol na feoiliteoirí, agus déanann sé iarracht freastal ar an uile dhúil dá bharr. Mar sin, cuireann sé feolta fuara ar fáil leis an tsailéad. An réimse sailéad, tá sé chomh buan lena fhoighne féin, lena fhlaithiúlacht agus lena chumas fíon maith a roghnú. Ar dhóigh eile, gan teorainn. Ach don fhoilseachán seo, níl ann ach glac beag. Lán glaice láimhe seacht méar, a deir sé.

Chickpea and Tuna | Sicphiseánach agus Tuinnín

This wonderfully tasty dish is best tackled from the dizzying heights of a high stool in the Horseshoe Bar. But beggars…….!!!!

The chickpeas? Depending on whether you have the time to steep and cook dried chickpeas in advance or if laziness or time constraints lead you to the canned variety it's all much of a oneness according to Ted.

So?

- Drained chickpeas
- Red onion
- Hard-boiled egg
- Can of 'no drain' tuna
- Salt and black pepper
- Chives or scallions * OPTIONAL
- Dressing

- *A good 'go' of drained chickpeas.*

- *Finely chopped red onion.*

- *Chopped hard-boiled egg.*

- *Can of 'no drain' tuna. Shred with two forks or just break up in the mixing.*

- *Salt and black pepper to season.*

- *Chopped chives or scallions optional.*

- *Place all ingredients in a large mixing bowl and mix with a wooden spoon or spatula.*

Add a dressing when serving. This can be as simple as a drizzle of olive oil and vinegar or the universal dressing set out at the end of the salad section.

This delicacy has an added advantage. It can be prepared a day in advance of a talks session or any other session.

Some wheaten bread wouldn't go amiss when you are serving it.

Smoked Mackerel Pâté | Pâté Murlais Dheataithe

- Smoked mackerel
- Red onion
- Salt and black pepper
- Lemon and/or lime juice
- Crème fraiche

Quick and easy.

🍴 *A quantity of Supermarket vacuum packed smoked mackerel de-skinned. Shred the meatier/firmer fish with two forks and zap the rest in a blender.*

🍴 *Some finely chopped red onion.*

🍴 *Salt, pepper and a go of lemon and/or lime juice according to taste.*

🍴 *A dollop of crème fraiche or mayonnaise.*

Place all ingredients in a bowl and mix with a spatula. When well combined, scoop into a bowl/container and press down. Decorate the top with thinly cut half slices of lemon.

This also can be prepared a day in advance.

Serve on a bread of your choice. The wheaten bread recipe in these pages works very well.

The Sinn Féin negotiating team favours this salad as a sustainer during long frustrating engagements, especially with the Democratic Unionist Party.

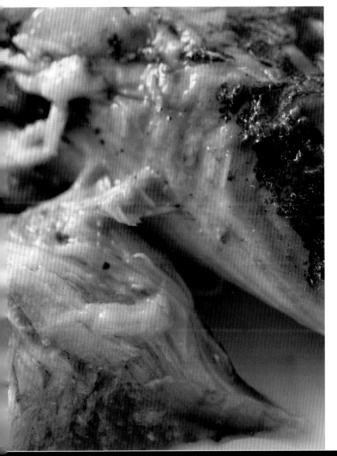

Photo by MaxStraeten at Morguefile.com

THE NEGOTIATORS COOK BOOK – BEST KEPT SECRET OF THE IRISH PEACE PROCESS

Potato Salad | Sailéad Prátaí

Potato Salad is good enough to constitute a lunch on its own; supplemented with some wheaten or crusty bread.

So?

- *A quantity of diced cooked salad potatoes. Waxy ones are best.*

- *Finely sliced table celery.*

- *Grated carrot.*

- *Finely chopped scallions.*

- *Finely chopped onion and hard-boiled eggs.*

- *Salt and pepper to season.*

- *Place all ingredients in a large bowl. Add a dollop of mayonnaise and mix. Put into a bowl/container and chill.*

Can be made the day before use.

- Salad potatoes
- Celery
- Carrot
- Scallions
- Onion
- Hard-boiled egg
- Salt and black pepper
- Mayonnaise

Photo by davidpwhelan at Morguefile.com

Celeriac Salad | Sailéad Soiliriace

A turnip-like thingy, Celeriac is available in many supermarkets nowadays.

Prepare in the same way as you would a turnip. Top, tail and remove the outer fibrous skin. Ted says Julienne what's left. To you and me that means slicing it into matchstick size strips.

- Celeriac
- Red onion
- Salt and pepper
- Lemon juice
- Mayonnaise
- Wholegrain mustard

Place julienned celeriac into a large bowl.

Season with salt, pepper and a squirt of lemon juice.

Lace a dollop of mayonnaise with a go of wholegrain mustard and mix well before adding to the celeriac.

Mix all ingredients together well and put in a bowl/container.

Can be prepared a day in advance.

Celerian Remoulaile is what they do in France. But sure what would they know!

Photo by pippalou at Morguefile.com

THE NEGOTIATORS COOK BOOK – BEST KEPT SECRET OF THE IRISH PEACE PROCESS

Beanz Salad | Sailéad Pónairí

Beanz?

Any one or all of the following: Cannellini, borlotti, red kidney, pinto.

It is too much hassle to steep and cook a mixture, so Ted advises that you stick to one variety. Otherwise go for a mix of canned beans which are available in most supermarkets.

So?

- *Beanz*
- *Finely chopped peppers/capsicums (two colours at least).*
- *Finely chopped Red onion.*
- *Table celery*
- *A can of corn niblets (drained).*
- *Place all ingredients in a bowl/container.*

When serving add a dressing of your choice. The 'universal' dressing described on page 34 works well.

- Cannellini, borlotti, red kidney or pinto beans
- Peppers/capsicums mixed
- Red onion
- Celery
- Can of sweetcorn
- Dressing

Photo by lisasolonynko at Morguefile.com

- Beetroot
- Crème fraiche
- Chives, scallion or parsley

Beetroot Salad | Sailéad Biatais

🍴 *Vacuum packed peeled and cooked beets are perfect.*

🍴 *Slice, add some seasoning and a dollop of crème fraiche tastefully dropped on the beetroot.*

🍴 *Add a pinch of something green for presentational purposes; Chopped chives, scallion or parsley work well.*

- Cos, Iceberg, Little gem lettuce, Radicchio, Spinach, or Rocket
- Cherry tomatoes
- Dressing

Green Salad | Sailéad Glas

Couldn't be simpler.

🍴 *Any GREENS or REDS for that matter either singly or in combination.*

🍴 *Cos, Iceberg, Little gem lettuce, Radicchio, Spinach, Rocket – whatever you are having yourself.*

🍴 *This plus a go of halved/quartered cherry tomatoes.*

A dressing (applied at point of serving) of your choice. The 'universal' dressing set out below works well.

Nota Bene: Segments of orange go well with any of the above. Also, alternatively, a drizzle of honey over some crumbled feta or goat's cheese. Far from it we was reared.

A Universal Dressing for Salads | Iastán Uilíoch le haghaidh Sailéad

- Olive oil
- White wine vinegar
- Lemon or Lime juice
- Mustard powder
- Garlic
- Basil, oregano or tarragon

What salads? Greens, beanz, chickpeas etc. as described already in this section.

The base?

🍴 *Half olive oil and one quarter white wine vinegar.*

🍴 *The other quarter? Lemon or lime juice or both.*

🍴 *Mustard powder.*

🍴 *Finely grated garlic.*

🍴 *A herb of your choice; basil, oregano, tarragon.*

Best prepared a day in advance. Shake well before applying to salad.

Photo by KodyKody1 at Morguefile.com

THE NEGOTIATORS COOK BOOK – BEST KEPT SECRET OF THE IRISH PEACE PROCESS

COLD CUTS FOR SALADS | FEOIL FHUAR LE HAGHAIDH SAILÉAD

The carnivores strike back. And, keep it simple. There is nothing more simple than boiled ham and poached chicken.

Tá na feoiliteoirí ar ais! Agus, coinnítear go simplí é. Níl a dhath ar bith níos simplí ná liamhás bruite agus sicín scallta.

Ham | Liamhás

With ham you get two for the price of one. That is, sliced cold gammon to accompany salads of your choice and a ham stock to make a flavoursome soup. Ted has thoughtfully provided a separate section on soups.

Cooking a bit of gammon?

- *Cover it with water. Bring to the boil.*
- *Remove any scum that comes to surface with a slotted spoon.*
- *Add a couple of bay leaves and some peppercorns.*
- *Cook for 1 - 2$^{1/2}$ hours according to weight i.e. 3lbs – 10lbs.*
- *Leave in a cold place to cool so it doesn't dehydrate.*
- *Remove from liquid and slice before serving*
- *Reserve the stock for soup.*

Photo by MaxStraeten at Morguefile.com

Chicken | Sicín

- Chicken breasts
- Stock flavouring * OPTIONAL
- Sage/rosemary
- Salt
- Black peppercorns
- Garlic

Chicken breasts, skinless and boneless, are widely available nowadays; may the Good Lord help us.

So?

We need to do something with it to make it work in taste terms. A vindaloo curry is one way. But poaching, which Ted recently stumbled into, is a better solution for gentler palates.

¶ *Cover chicken breasts in a wide, deep pot with water. The addition of one of them gellied stock thingys is entirely acceptable.*

¶ *Add herb/s of choice: Sage leaves, rosemary sprigs.*

¶ *Some salt, black peppercorns.*

¶ *A whole clove or two of garlic.*

¶ *Bring to the boil and simmer for 20/25 minutes.*

¶ *Remove from heat and allow to cool in the cooking liquor before slicing for salads.*

¶ *Freeze stock if not using at the time.*

Mustards/chutneys will enhance the above cold cuts of ham and chicken.

STOCKS | STOIC

The basis of any good soup is a good quality stock. After that it's difficult to go wrong.

Ted doesn't do beef stock. He says its too expensive for an orphaned, single parent, widow man pensioner. He does ham and chicken stock.

Is bunús aon anraith maith stoc den scoth. Ina dhiaidh sé, tá deacair dul chun donais.

Ní bhacann Ted le stoc mairteola. Deir sé go bhfuil sé ródhaor do bhaintreach fir ar tuismitheoir aonair é, ar fágadh ina dhílleachta é agus atá anois ar scor. Pléann sé le stoc liamháis agus stoc sicín.

Ham Stock | Stoc Liamháis this stock makes itself. Boil a gammon and Bob's yer Uncle. Couldn't be simpler. See cold cuts on page 35 and 36

Photo by auttiedot at Morguefile.com

- Chicken * WHATEVER CUT IS AVAILABLE
- Onion
- Celery
- Carrot
- Peppercorns
- Salt
- Greens from cauliflour
- Stalks of mushrooms
- Stalk of broccoli

Chicken Stock | Stoc Sicín

Use chicken wings or drumsticks or any chicken you come across in the supermarket on sale with a that day or next day sell by date.

🍴 *Cover with cold water. Bring to the boil. Remove impurities with a slotted spoon.*

🍴 *Add sliced onion, celery, carrots, peppercorns, bay leaves, salt and anything else you have.*

🍴 *Add the greens from a cauliflour, stalks of mushrooms, stalk of broccoli trimmed of its fibrous skin.*

🍴 *Simmer for 2 - 2½ hours.*

🍴 *Sieve - remove the flavour spent chicken and veg.*

Happy Souping!

Photo by beglib at Morguefile.com

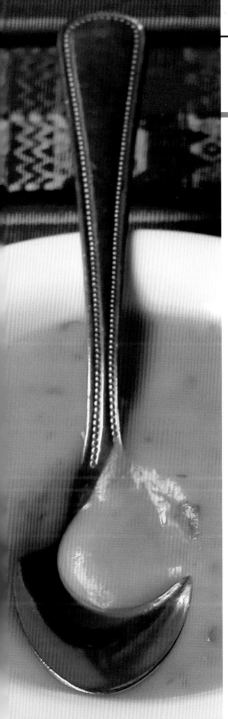

SOUPS | ANRAITHÍ

'They took the soup' used to be a judgemental way of describing those who were perceived to have acquiesced to the system. Or those who actually did so. It comes from the time of The Great Hunger in 1845-1850-ish. Soup Kitchens were established in some parts of our little island during that terrible time of An Gorta Mór. While some of these soup kitchens may have been set up as acts of charity, in others soup was dispensed only to those prepared to anglicise their native names. Or so Ted tells me.

'Ghlac siad leis an sú' a deirtí chun breithiúnas a thabhairt orthu siúd a measadh a ghéill don chóras. Nó, leoga, leo siúd a ghéill dáiríre. Tagann sé chugainn ó ré an Ghorta Mhóir 1845-1850, nó mar sin. Bunaíodh tithe anraith in áiteanna ar fud ár n-oileáin bhig le linn bhlianta an drochshaoil. Cé gur bunaíodh cuid acu ar bhonn carthanais, b'fhéidir, ní thugadh cuid acu aon sú ach dóibh sin a bhí sásta a n-ainmneacha dúchais a ghalldú. Sin an méid a deir Ted liom, cibé.

Coole, high steeple
Poor town and proud people
They sold their souls
For penny rolls
For soup and hairy bacon.

Photo by clarita at Morguefile.com

So it is true that we took the soup, in Stormont of all places, but it was Ted's soup. Unconditionally subversive, hearty and sustaining. And usually green. Or red.

Time constraints and the eccentric appetites amongst the Negotiating Team on the Hill make simple soup a necessity. A good stock makes this possible. Ted comes from good stock. McCoys from Rathlin Island, Elmores from Omeath, McFaddens from Glenarm and Howells from Stratford on Avon in England. A quare mix.

Is fíor, mar sin, gur ghlac muid leis an sú, ar Chnoc an Anfa thar áit ar bith eile; ach ba le Ted an sú seo. Ceannairceach gan choinníoll, go breá is go cothaitheach. Agus de dhath glas, de ghnáth. Nó dearg.

Easpa ama agus goilí saoithiúla i measc na foirne idirbheartaíochta ar an Chnoc, d'fhág siad sin an sú simplí ina dhíol riachtanach. Déanann stoc maith mar bhunús an chúis. Tagann Ted ó shliocht maith mar bhunús. McCoys in Oileán Reachlainn, Elmores ón Ó Meith, Mac Pháidín Ghleann Arma agus Howells ó Stratford on Avon i Sasana. Meascán ceart.

Photo by MaxStraeten at Morguefile.com

From Ham Stock | Ón stoc liamháis

Red Lentil/Tomato & Rice | Lintile rua/tráta agus rís

- Red lentils
- Brown rice
- Onion
- Carrot
- French beans
- Tin of tomatoes or passata
- Chilli * OPTIONAL

- Red lentils and brown rice.

- Wash all of the above well.

- Add the ham stock, finely chopped onion, carrot and french beans.

- Add a can of chopped tomatoes or a carton of passata.

- A small chilli will provide a pleasant background heat.

- Season to taste and cook until everything is done.

Green Pea | Pis Glas

- Split green peas
- Onion
- Carrot
- Gammon
- Garlic sausage

- Soak split green peas overnight.

- Bring to the boil in the ham stock.

- Remove impurities with slotted spoon.

- Add finely chopped carrot and onion.

- Shred and add any bits of gammon that might be available.

- Add sliced garlic sausage and you get the Dutch national dish.

- Onion
- Carrot
- Celery
- Courgette
- Green pepper
- Green beans
- Tin of tomatoes or passata
- Pasta
- Beans – red kidney/pinto/ borlotti

Photo by clarita at Morguefile.com

From Chicken Stock | Ón stoc sicín

Minestrone | Mineastróine

Ted remembers, and he claims he's not good at that this weather, hearing that there are two types of this soup. One from Northern Italy where they do beans. The other from the South where they do pasta. All embracing soul that Ted is he does both.

Is cuimhin le Ted, agus maíonn sé nach bhfuil cuimhne mhaith aige ar an aimsir seo, is cuimhin leis gur chuala sé áit éigin go bhfuil dhá shaghas den anraith seo ann. Ceann amháin ó thuaisceart na hIodáile mar a n-úsáideann siad pónairí. An ceann eile is as deisceart na tíre sin mar a n-úsáideann siad pasta. Mar fhear uileghabhálach, déanann Ted an dá rud.

As usual the good quality stock is key. To this add:

🍴 *Finely diced carrot, onion, celery, courgette, green pepper, green beans.*

🍴 *Add a can or two of chopped tomatoes or carton's of passata.*

🍴 *For the last 15/20 minutes of cooking add broken pasta (e.g. spaghetti) or small pasta like Orzo, plus cooked beanz of choice – red kidney/ pinto/borlotti.*

🍴 *Season to taste.*

Potato and Leek |
Cainneann agus prátaí

Add to the chicken stock:

- Rooster potatoes
- Onion
- Leeks
- Green beans
- Carrot
- Cannellini beans

🍴 *Rooster spuds*

🍴 *Sliced onion*

🍴 *Finely sliced leeks.*

🍴 *Cook and blitz with a hand held blender.*

🍴 *Season to taste.*

Enhance with a can or two of cannellini beans or some finely sliced green beans or shredded carrot cooked separately.

Photo by MaxStraeten at Morguefile.com

Courgette & Tomato | Cúirséad agus Tráta

To the chicken stock add:

- *Sliced courgettes*
- *Onion*
- *Tomatoes (tins)*
- *Carrot*
- *A sensible amount of turmeric*
- *Blitz with a hand held blender*
- *A couple of rooster spuds can be included in the above for a thicker consistency.*
- *Season to taste.*

- Courgettes
- Onion
- Tins of tomatoes
- Carrot
- Turmeric
- Rooster potatoes * OPTIONAL

Photo by versionx7 at Morguefile.com

BEANZ | PÓNAIRÍ

VARIETIES | SÓIRT

🍴 **Dried | Triomaithe**

🍴 **Canned (for salads or hot dishes) | Stánaithe**

🍴 **Beans and Sausage | Pónairí agus Ispíní**

🍴 **Beans and Chicken | Pónairí agus Sicín**

🍴 **Beans and Pork | Pónairí agus Muiceoil**

In my opinion, beans on their own are as good as it gets for protein and energy, for lunch or dinner. Or, supplemented with chicken, pork, or shrimps, they're a meal and a half.

I mo thuairim féin, tá pónairí leo féin chomh maith is a gheofá don phróitéin agus don fhuinneamh, am lóin nó am dinnéir. Sin nó sicín, muiceoil nó séaclaí a chur leis, agus is béile faoi leith a bheidh agat.

What beanz?

Cannellini, Borlotti, Pinto, Red kidney. Or for that matter chickpeas. Dried and tinned varieties are available in most supermarkets now.

DRIED: Soak for 8 hours, either overnight or before leaving home in the morning. Boil/simmer for 1 - 1½ hours removing any froth or scum in the process before adding some black peppercorns and bay leaves.

CANNED: (No smart Alex remarks) Just drain and you're good to go. Use either a single variety or mixed in any preferred combination.

So?

Once you have cooked beanz or chickpeas the rest is easy. You have a basis for cold salads or hot dishes. Chick pea and tuna salad and bean salad are set out on pages 28 and 32.

For a hot dish the starting point is a basic tomato sauce (sort of basic):

Sautée finely chopped smoked streaky bacon, onion and garlic.

Add canned tomatoes or carton/s of passata.

Add finely chopped carrot, celery, green pepper/capsicum, a bay leaf or two, a small hot red/green pepper if you have one to hand.

And then? Whatever floats your boat!

- Smoked streaky bacon
- Onion
- Garlic
- Tin of tomatoes or passata
- Carrot
- Celery
- Green pepper
- Bay leaf
- Hot red/green chilli * OPTIONAL

I like sausages. In supermarkets these days there's plenty or at least enough available; chorizo, smoked pork, lots of good Polish sausages, Whatever you fancy and, amount wise, according to the numbers you are feeding.

Beyond that? Herb/s of choice! Cooked chicken, shrimps or whatever tickles your fancy or your palate.

Pork and Beanz: Best to season loin of pork chops or pork steaks on both sides and braise gently until cooked/tender. And then add the beans to the heat.

Serve any of the above either as they come or with a bread of choice – crusty stuff is good – or on a bed of rice.

Photo by puravida at Morguefile.com

THE NEGOTIATORS COOK BOOK – BEST KEPT SECRET OF THE IRISH PEACE PROCESS

Photo by snowbear at Morguefile.com

PIES | PIÓGA

 **Ham & Leek** | **Liamhás agus Cainneann**

Chicken & Leek | **Sicín agus Cainneann**

Cottage Pie | **Pióg an Aoire**

Pies: Couldn't be simpler. See the COLD CUT recipes for gammon and chicken set out in pages 35 and 36. These cooked meats are the basis for two comfort food pies.

Ham & Leek Pie | Liamhás agus Cainneann

- Cooked ham
- Cooking liquor/stock
- Button mushrooms
- Leek
- Onion
- Butter
- Olive Oil
- Crème fraiche
- Shortcrust pastry
- Egg wash

¶ *Dice the cooked ham.*

¶ *Add a small amount of the cooking liquor/stock along with some small or quartered button mushrooms. Place in a large bowl.*

¶ *Sauteé some thinly sliced leeks and onion in olive oil and butter and tip into the chicken, mushroom, stock.*

¶ *Mix together.*

¶ *Add a judicious dollop of crème fraiche. Judicious? Less rather than more. You can add but it's more difficult to take away. Too much liquid will give your pie a 'soggy bottom'. (Which reminds me. Get the soundtrack of 'Oh Brother Where Art Thou' and the best of Appalachian music from the Soggy Bottom Boys.)*

¶ *Line a pie dish with the shortcrust pastry. Supermarket shortcrust and puff pastry perfect for this.*

¶ *Line a pie dish with the shortcrust pastry.*

¶ *Tip in the chicken and leek filling.*

¶ *Cover with the puff pastry and seal the edges with finger and thumbs or a spoon/fork.*

¶ *Give the surface a beaten egg wash and use a fork/skewer to put some air holes in the surface of the pie.*

¶ *Bake in a pre-heated oven 180°Fahrenheit for 35/40 minutes until the pastry is done.*

Chicken & Leek Pie | Sicín agus Cainneann

Exactly the same as above but with chicken instead of ham. Add a drop of tarragon to the filling if you wish. But use sparingly. It's strong.

Cottage Pie | Pióg an Aoire

Equally simple.

- Sauteé finely chopped onion and garlic.

- Add minced steak and brown it.

- Put in one or two gellied stock thingys and then a can of chopped tomatoes.

- Some Worcestershire sauce and dry mustard powder helps.

- Then a drop of water accompanied by finely chopped carrot and finely sliced celery.

- Use enough water to cook the vegetables but watch the 'soggy bottom' syndrome.

- Season to taste when the filling is nearly done

- If necessary reduce the liquid in the process.

- Cool the meat and tip into a pie dish.

- Cover with cold mashed potatoes (roosters are the best for this) which has been seasoned and mixed with a dollop of crème fraiche or milk.

- Reheat well in a micro wave oven.

- Onion
- Garlic
- Minced steak
- Stock jelly/cube
- Worcestershire sauce
- Mustard powder
- Carrot
- Celery
- Mashed potatoes
- Crème fraiche

Photo by MaxStraeten at Morguefile.com

THE NEGOTIATORS COOK BOOK – BEST KEPT SECRET OF THE IRISH PEACE PROCESS

MAINS | PRÍOMHCHÚRSAÍ

- Chicken 'n' Pasta | Sicín is Pasta
- Beef Paprika | Paiprice Muiceola
- Chilli McCarney | Sillí Mhic Cearnaigh
- Pork and Apricot Curry | Curaí Muiceola is Aibreoga

Mains: The constraints of microwave reheating is the main determinant here. Ach, c'est la vie as we say in Ballymurphy.

Photo by ariadna at Morguefile.com

Chicken 'n' Pasta | Sicín is Pasta

Quick and simple.

🍴 *Sauteé finely chopped onion and garlic.*

🍴 *Add diced or sliced chicken breasts to seal the meat.*

🍴 *Add, after 10/15 minutes, sliced or diced peppers (2 or 3 different colours).*

Then? Whatever tickles your fancy?

Options: Lemon and coriander;

🍴 *Quarter a lemon and add with the capsicums as well as some fresh or dry coriander (or oregano for that matter).*

🍴 *Then, when cooked, a dollop of crème fraiche.*

Tomato and basil:

🍴 *Add a can of chopped tomatoes, tomato puree, fresh or dried basil when adding the capsicums. (Thirty minutes cooking with either option is plenty).*

The Pasta | An Pasta: Whatever you have or whatever you prefer. All are quick to cook. So take your pick. Unlike me, Ted prefers Gnocchi – available fresh or vacuum packed in most supermarkets and it cooks in minutes in boiling water. Rigatoni, Penne and pastas of that size take marginally longer. Cook, drain, add a drizzle of olive oil while still warm and add to the chicken.

Alternatively serve the chicken on a bed of rice.

- Onion
- Garlic
- Chicken breasts
- Peppers mix

Option I
- Lemon
- Coriander/oregano
- Crème fraiche

Option II
- Tin of tomatoes
- Tomato puree
- Basil

- Pasta of choice
- Olive oil

Beef Paprika | Paiprice Muiceola

Ted uses three different paprikas for this dish; sweet, smoked and hot. But any one or combination of these does the job.

- ¶ *Sauteé some finely chopped onion and garlic and set to the side.*

- ¶ *Get a plastic bag without holes.*

- ¶ *Put in a tablespoon full of plain flour, salt, pepper and a good go of paprika.*

- ¶ *Twist the neck of the bag to seal and shake to mix.*

- ¶ *Add the beef, diced. Whatever you normally use for stews and casseroles. Steak pieces/chuck steak/plate steak or whatever.*

- ¶ *Twist the neck of the bag again and shake to coat the beef in the flour/seasoning/paprika mixture.*

- ¶ *Let the flour settle for a minute.*

- ¶ *Remove the beef, shaking off the excess flour coating and set to the side.*

- ¶ *Hold onto the extra flour in the plastic bag.*

- ¶ *In a casserole dish brown the beef pieces in small batches in whatever oil you normally use.*

- ¶ *When finished return all the beef/onion and garlic to the casserole.*

- ¶ *Add the reserved flour/paprika a bit at a time stirring constantly to cook the flour for both thickening and flavouring the sauce.*

¶ Add a can of chopped tomatoes/passata, stirring constantly to combine with the beef/flour etc.

¶ Adjust the liquid to enable cooking.

¶ Add French green beans sliced lengthwise or on the diagonal.

¶ Some sliced mushrooms would be good.

¶ Cook/simmer 'til tender making sure liquid content is monitored to prevent burning.

¶ Serve on a bed of rice.

- Onion
- Garlic
- Paprika - sweet, smoked or hot - all or any
- Plain flour
- Salt
- Pepper
- Beef
- Tin of tomatoes or passata
- French green beans
- Mushrooms

Photo by szafirek at Morguefile.com

Photo by aborfromHungary at Morguefile.com

THE NEGOTIATORS COOK BOOK – BEST KEPT SECRET OF THE IRISH PEACE PROCESS

"Chilli McCarney" | "Sillí Mhic Cearnaigh"

According to Ted this is a west of Ireland dish created by Dáithí McCarney and his Mexican wife, Rosalita. While not as widely known as the more famous Irish stew it is renowned in all good eating houses west of the Shannon. And the Bann. The renowned cook Kenny Floyd said, "If it had been invented in France Chilli McCarney would be on the menu of every good restaurant in the world." Kenny was known to take a wee drink or two. But regardless, Dáithí McCarney has ensured that Ireland will take our place among the kitchens of the world. For their part he and Rosalita deserve culinary recognition world-wide. Ted and I salute their achievement.

Dar le Ted, is de bhunadh iarthar na hÉireann an sampla seo; ceann a chruthaigh Dáithí McCarney agus a bhean chéile Rosalita, ar Meicsiceach í. Cé nach bhfuil sé chomh haitheanta céanna leis an stobhach chlúiteach Ghaelach, tá cáil air i ngach bialann mhaith taobh ó thiar den tSionainn. Agus den Bhanna. Dúirt an cócaire clúiteach Kenny Floyd. "dá gcruthófaí sa Fhrainc é, bheadh sé ar fáil i ngach bialann mhaith ar dhroim an domhain". Tá sé amuigh air go raibh dúil aige san ól. Ina dhiaidh sin féin, tá cinntithe anois ag Dáithí McCarney go mbeidh ár n-áit againn mar Éirinn i measc chistineacha na cruinne. Mar gheall air féin agus ar Rosalita, tá aitheantas idirnáisiúnta cócaireachta tuillte acu. Tugann muid, mise agus Ted, ómós don méid atá bainte amach acu.

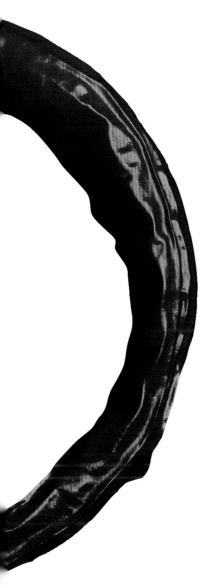

And so to business: Chilli McCarney:

- *Sauteé finely diced onion and garlic for a few minutes.*

- *Lower the heat and add a good go of paprika – sweet or smoked.*

- *Add a heaped teaspoon of cumin and*

- *3/4 of a teaspoon of chilli powder.*

- *Cook gently, stirring continuously for 2/3 minutes.*

- *Add minced steak and continue to stir until coloured and separated.*

- *The ubiquitous chopped tomatoes/passata, tomato puree and seasoning.*

- *Add finely chopped carrot and after a time diced pepper/capsicum.*

- *Cook until carrots/peppers are done.*

- *Add drained and rinsed cans of kidney or pinto beans, corn niblets and taste for seasoning.*

- *Serve on a bed of rice – I use brown- with, optionally, a dollop of soured cream or crème fraiche.*

- Onion
- Garlic
- Paprika - sweet or smoked
- Cumin
- Chilli powder
- Minced steak
- Tin of tomatoes or passata
- Carrots
- Pepper/capsicum.
- Kidney or pinto beans
- Sweetcorn
- Soured cream or crème fraiche

Nota Bene: This recipe works equally well with chicken. Instead of minced steak use chicken breasts. Cube or cut into strips/seal on a warm pan and add to the chilli sauce. Cook for 15/20 minutes.

Nota eile: Dáithí McCarney died from an overdose of tall yarns in 1948. Rosalita lives in a suburb of Mexico City. She is now a hundred and sixteen years of age and is on her fourth husband. That's women for you.

Photo by hotblack at Morguefile.com

Pork and Apricot Curry (Kwik variety) | Curaí Muiceola is Aibreoga

- Onion
- Pork
- Jar of curry sauce
- Coconut milk/cream
- Apricots or peach halves
- Lemon juice

Sauteé thinly sliced onion.

Add diced pork steak to seal.

Follow this with some water and simmer until tender.

Add a jar/s of a curry sauce of your choice and coconut milk or cream.

In parallel with the above process drain a can/s of apricots or peach halves.

Rinse the fruit and add some lemon juice to it in a bowl.

Add to the pork curry to heat through

Serve on a bed of rice.

Photo by imelenchon at Morguefile.com

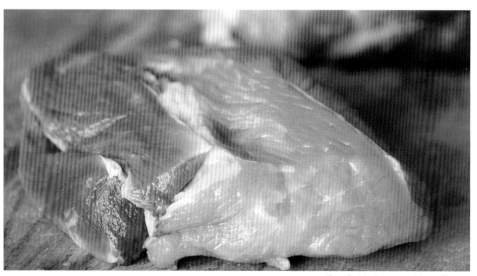

Photo by MaxStraeten at Morguefile.com

DESSERTS | MILSEOGA

The majority of these recipes come from Pádraic Wilson's granny, Josie Woods, and through her to his mammy, Maureen Wilson. They are old favourites associated with Easter, Christmas and Halloween. The desserts not his Mammy or Granny Woods.

Pádraic doesn't confine his delious delights to special times. He is just as happy making them at any time. Pádraic is an ancient Romantic. He is also pre-metric. These special treats are made, by him, using the old measurements. He claims this adds to the sense of nostalgia. The smells and aromas are magic. So is Pádraic. I don't remember exactly when he started bringing his sweet offerings to Stormont. I do remember him arriving at our house at set times like Christmas with wonderful cakes. His Christmas puddings are legendary. They also last for years. It's the alcohol in them. Anyway sometimes the only sweet thing at Stormont was a Pádraic Pudding. Just the perfect finish to a Ted lunch. He has provided us with some samples of his creativity. Long live his Granny Josie and his Mammy Maureen. Long live Pádraic. Here is one of his simply made puddings.

Tagann an chuid is mó de na hoidis seo ó Josie Woods, máthair mhór Phádraic Wilson; uaithi sin chuig a mháthair Maureen Wilson, agus anuas chugainn féin. Seanroghanna coitianta is ea iad, roghanna a bhaineann leis an Cháisc, leis an Nollaig nó le hOíche Shamhna. Is é sin gur seanroghanna coitianta na milseoga. Ní hé a Mhamaí nó Mamó Woods atá i gceist.

Ní choinníonn Pádraic a chuidse…do hócáidí speisialta amháin. Tá sé chomh sásta céanna iad a dhéanamh in am ar bith. Is seanrómánsaí é Pádraic. Is de bhunadh na ré méadraí é freisin. Déanann seisean na rudaí speisialta seo trí úsáid a bhaint as an tseanchóras. Maíonn sé go gcuireann sé leis an chumha i ndiaidh an tseansaoil. Tá an dea-bholadh go hiontach. Mar atá Pádraic. Ní cuimhin liom go díreach cá huair a thosaigh sé ag tabhairt na mbronntanas milis seo chuig Stormont. Sin ráite, is cuimhin liom é ag teacht chuig an teach s'againne ag amanna áirithe, ar nós na Nollag, agus cístí iontacha ina ghlac aige. Tá na maróga Nollag mór le rá aige. Maireann siad na blianta. Sin an t-alcól atá iontu. Cibé ar bith, uaireanta ar Chnoc an Anfa, ba í maróg de chuid Phádraic an t-aon rud milis a bhíodh le fáil. Deireadh foirfe sásúil le lón à la Ted. Tá roinnt samplaí dá chruthaitheacht curtha ar fáil aige anseo dúinn. Gura fada buan a Mhamó Josie agus a Mhamaí Maureen. Gura fada buan Pádraic. Seo a leanas ceann de na maróga atá simplí a dhéanamh.

Apple Crumble | Mionbhruar Úll

Preheat the oven to 190°c

- 8ozs Plain or self-raising flour
- 4ozs Margarine (room temperature)
- 6ozs Caster sugar
- Pinch of salt
- 3-4 Cooking apples
- Sugar (plain, cinnamon or demerara)
- Custard or ice-cream (or both)

Mix the flour and salt.

Rub in the margarine with your hands until it resembles breadcrumbs.

Stir in the sugar.

Peel and core 3-4 cooking apples. Pádraic says the number of apples you use really depends how deep you want the filling. I like my fillings as deep as can be.

Slice the apples and layer them in a suitable oven dish.

Sprinkle with sugar – it's a matter of taste whether you use plain, cinnamon or demerara.

Cover the apples with the crumble mix.

Bake in the oven for 25-30 minutes at 190°c. Serve hot or cold with your favourite side – custard or ice-cream. I have both!

Photo by MaxStraeten at Morguefile.com

THE NEGOTIATORS COOK BOOK – BEST KEPT SECRET OF THE IRISH PEACE PROCESS

Flaky Pastry *(For sweet OR savoury)* | **Taosrán Calógach**

- 6ozs butter (soft)
- 8ozs plain flour
- Pinch of salt.
- I egg, beaten.

Add the butter to the flour and salt in a mixing bowl. Mix by hand until it resembles breadcrumbs.

Add the beaten egg.

Mix with a knife until it forms into a dough. The dough should be smooth and not stiff.

Add a little drop of cold water if the dough is too stiff.

Knead the dough a little, then wrap in greaseproof paper and allow to rest in the fridge for at least an hour. It can be frozen for use later.

When ready to use, preheat the oven to 220°c (Gas Mark 7)

The dough can be used for almost any type of tart/pie. The filling is a matter of personal choice.

Cut off a slightly larger bit of dough.

Roll it out on a board or surface dusted with flour. Make sure the rolled dough is big enough to cover the surface of the tart/pie dish.

The base should be slightly thicker than the top. Grease the dish or plate. Trim any excess pastry. Add the filling.

Photo by MaxStraeten at Morguefile.com

THE NEGOTIATORS COOK BOOK – BEST KEPT SECRET OF THE IRISH PEACE PROCESS

Apple Tart | Toirtín Úll

We always called it Apple cake in our house but whatever it's called this is one of my favourite desserts. My Aunt Annie made a mean apple cake. Ted does a Dutch version which is very nice but Pádraic is an Apple baker supreme. This is how he does it.

Císte Úll a thugtaí air i gcónaí i dteach s'againne, ach cibé rud a thugtar air tá sé ar na milseoga is ansa liom. Dhéanadh m'aintín Annie sárchíste úll. Déanann Ted leagan deas Ísiltíreach – ach is sainbháicéir úll é Pádraic. Seo mar a dhéanann:

- Slice the peeled and cored cooking apples.

- Sprinkle the layered apples with sugar – try cinnamon sugar.

- Roll out the remaining dough. Lay it over the fruit filled base. Trim any excess dough.

- Seal the edges by pressing down with your thumbs. Cut a few slits on top to release steam. Brush the top with milk.

- Bake in the oven at 220°c for 25-30 minutes.

- Sprinkle with sugar on top when you take it out of the oven (try demerara).

- Flaky pastry
- Cooking apples.
- Sugar (cinnamon/demerara)
- Milk

Photo by kandi at Morguefile.com

THE NEGOTIATORS COOK BOOK – BEST KEPT SECRET OF THE IRISH PEACE PROCESS

Chocolate Sponge | Císte Spúinse Seacláide

Preheat the oven to 190°c (Gas Mark 5)

- 8ozs Self-raising flour
- Cocoa powder (replace 2-3 dessert spoons of flour with same of cocoa powder)
- Pinch of salt.
- 8ozs Caster sugar
- 8ozs Margarine (Room Temp)
- 4 Eggs

In a mixer cream the margarine and sugar. If you want a work-out, do it by hand.

Add the eggs.

Sieve the flour/cocoa/salt into a bowl.

Add in small batches, at a low speed. Once all the flour mix has been added, increase the speed. (You can, of course, add it all at once at high speed. This is only good craic if there are grand kids about – otherwise it's a pain to clean up!)

Mix until it is light and airy.

Grease or line, with greaseproof or parchment paper, two suitable cake tins. (8" tins are best).

Pour the mixture into the tins.

Bake in the oven for 25-30 minutes at 190°c.

Remove from the oven and tap out each tin onto a cooling rack.

Gently remove the paper.

When completely cooled spread the filling over the top of one cake and set the other on top. (For suggested filling and or topping see buttercream recipe on page 62).

Photo by MaxStraeten at Morguefile.com

THE NEGOTIATORS COOK BOOK – BEST KEPT SECRET OF THE IRISH PEACE PROCESS

Butter Cream Filling | Líonadh Uachtair Ime

🍴 Cream the butter and icing sugar. You can do it in a mixer at a low speed.

🍴 Add the vanilla seeds.

🍴 If the mixture is a bit stiff, add a little milk - be careful not too much!

🍴 You can use the cream to fill a chocolate sponge. Replace 2-3 spoonfuls of icing sugar with cocoa powder for a "chocolate" cream.

- 4ozs Butter (soft)
- 6ozs Icing sugar
- 1 Vanilla pod (deseeded)
  * OPTIONAL

For a Chocolate Cake Topping | Barrán Seacláide le haghaidh cáca

🍴 Melt a bar or two of your favourite chocolate in a heat proof bowl over some hot water in a pot.

🍴 Once the chocolate has melted remove from the heat.

🍴 Spread the chocolate over the top of the cake or all over it if you've melted enough chocolate,

Allow it to cool, then get stuck in.

- Bar or two of your favourite chocolate

Císte na Nollaig

Margaret Mulhern makes my favourite Christmas cake but I'm sure she would approve of Pádraic's recipe. He never actually brought any of it to our team as far as I can recall but I include it because it's a good cake to make or eat and in memory of the Christmas when they all deserted me and I spent most of the festive season on the phone trying to get Tony Blair to do the right thing. Again. But that's another story. Over to you P.

Déanann Margaret Mulhern an císte Nollag is fearr liom féin. Ach tá mé cinnte de go mbeadh sí sásta le hoideas Phadraic. Níor thug sé don fhoireann s'againne é ar chor ar bith, dé réir mo chuimhne, ach tá sé san áireamh anseo nó is cáca maith é le hithe nó le hullmhú. Is rud maith é in ómós don Nollaig fosta, nuair a thréig siad mé, nuair a chaith mé an chuid is mó de shéasúr na Nollag in ….. ag iarraidh ar Tony Blair an rud ceart a dhéanamh. Ach sin scéal eile. Ar aghaidh leat P.

Preheat the oven to 160c (Gas mark 3).

Cream the margarine and brown sugar in a bowl.

Sieve, into a bowl, the flour, nutmeg, cream of tartar, mixed spice and salt mix.

Add to creamed mix.

Add the eggs one at a time to the mix.

Add the fruit (including the lemon juice and the zest) and brandy.

Recent years, courtesy of Ted and Marty, Pádraic has favoured Macieira. That's because he gets it free gratias and for nothing. Maceira is a Portugese brandy. I am partial to it myself. That's also because I get it for nothing although so far only from Ted and big Bob. Two gentlemen.

Mix well, by hand at this stage, with a wooden spoon.

The overall mixture will make enough for approximately one 7lb cake or a 3lb and a 4lb set.

Make sure you know the weight of the cake(s) you are baking, as it will dictate the time in the oven.

Line the base and sides of the cake tin(s) with greaseproof or parchment paper.

- 1lb Margarine (room temperature)
- 1lb Soft brown sugar (light or dark)
- 1lb Raisins
- 1 1/2lbs Sultanas (you can replace 1/2lb with currants if ye like)
- 1/2lb Cherries, halved (glacé)
- 1 1/2lbs Plain flour
- 10 Eggs
- 2 teaspoons Mixed Spice
- 1/4 teaspoon Nutmeg (ground)
- 1 egg spoon Cream of Tartar
- Zest and juice of one lemon (make sure the zest is finely grated or chopped)
- Pinch of salt
- 3 tablespoons of brandy – or more if you want

🍴 *Add the mixture to the tin(s).*

🍴 *Pat down in the tin gently (dampen the back of the fingers of one hand with milk) and make a slight indentation in the centre.*

🍴 *Bake for 1 hour for the first pound weight at 160°c and $^1/_2$ hour at 150°c for each additional pound.*

🍴 *Towards the end of baking time insert a skewer into the centre of the cake – if it comes out dry – it's done.*

* **As ovens can vary it's best to check coming up to the last five or ten minutes so just to be sure, to be sure.**

🍴 *Allow to cool slightly, then remove from the tin(s) onto a cooling rack.*

🍴 *It can be eaten when cooled, but it's best to wrap in tin foil, when cooled completely, and let it rest for a few days. If properly sealed it will keep for a few weeks.*

🍴 *You can sprinkle some more brandy over the top, to keep it, and you, topped up.*

It can be eaten as is or covered in marzipan and icing – recipes included.

- *3/4*lb White bread crumbs
- *1/2*lb (Atora) Suet
- 2lbs Fruit (sultanas, cherries, raisins)
- *1/2*lb lb Soft brown sugar
- Large teaspoon mixed spice
- Large teaspoon nutmeg (ground)
- Zest & juice of 2 lemons (finely grate the zest)
- 6 eggs, beaten
- 2 Tablespoons brandy (more, if desired, which it is!)

Maróg na Nollaig

This is my favourite Pádraic offering. My Christmas would be incomplete without his Christmas Pudding.

Seo an ceann le Pádraic is fearr liom. Nollaig easnamhach a bheadh ann in éagumais a Mharóig Nollag.

To make your own you need to:

- *Mix all ingredients, except the eggs and brandy, together in a bowl.*
- *Add the beaten eggs and brandy last (Once again Ted & Marty's Macieira).*
- *This will make 1 good 4lb pudding or 2 good 2lb efforts.*
- *Put the mixture into an appropriate sized pudding bowl(s).*
- *Place a piece of greaseproof paper over the mixture before putting the lid on or sealing it. If I'm using a bowl with no lid, I simply cover it with tin-foil and tie it in place with string.*
- *Have a pot big enough to take the bowl.*
- *Bring water to the boil. Place the pudding bowl in the pot (the sealed/lid upwards)*
- *Boil for 1 hour per pound.*
- *Keep checking the water level and top up as required.*
- *Don't submerge the bowl!*
- *Once boiled and cooled, the pudding will keep for ages. I usually seal it all over with cling film.*

Marzipan *(Almond Paste)* |
Prásóg *(Leafaos Almóinní)*

- 1lb Icing sugar
- 1lb Ground almonds
- 2 medium eggs, beaten
- Lemon juice (*1/2* lemon)
- 1 teaspoon Almond essence

- Mix the sugar and almonds in a bowl.

- Add the lemon juice and almond essence.

- Add the beaten eggs; mix with a wooden spoon to a stiff paste.

- Knead until well mixed.

- Dust a suitable board/surface with icing sugar and roll out the desired amount.

- This mixture will top several cakes or completely cover one – depends on how you want to decorate it/them.

- **Brush the surface of the cake with egg white before putting on the marzipan. Otherwise it won't stay!**

Dust the covered cake with icing sugar and allow it to sit 2-3 days before icing.

Icing | Reoán

- 3/4 - 1lb of icing sugar
- Egg white
- Juice of a lemon

- Add the egg white and lemon juice to the icing sugar in a bowl and mix with a wooden spoon.

- It takes a bit of effort, but it will fairly quickly form into a thick icing sugar.

- If it is too loose add a little more icing sugar until it thickens.

To be safe start off with 3/4lb and add a little more as needed.

- Once satisfied with the mixture, use a pallet knife to spread over the top of the cake or if entirely covered in marzipan then go for it.

- To smooth the finished article, warm the pallet knife in warm water and smooth out the icing.

Leave for a few days and decorate if you wish.

Panacotta

- 600 mls Double cream
- 150 mls Full milk
- 1 Vanilla pod, split
- 150g Sugar
- 5 Gelatine leaves

🍴 *Heat the milk, cream, sugar and vanilla pods in a pot on a low heat. Do not boil.*

🍴 *Soak the gelatine leaves in cold water. When the leaves have soaked, squeeze any excess water and add to the hot cream mixture. Stir until the gelatine has dissolved.*

🍴 *Pass the mixture through a sieve to remove the vanilla pods.*

🍴 *Pour into suitable bowls/glasses and let them set in the fridge.*

Strawberry Sauce/Topping | Anlann/ Barrán Sú Talún

- 400g Strawberries
- 50mls Water (cold).
- 75g Sugar
- 1 Vanilla pod, split.
- 1 inch of lemon skin approximately (no rind)
- 5 gelatine leaves

🍴 *Heat the water and sugar on a low heat.*

🍴 *Add the vanilla pod and lemon skin.*

🍴 *When the sugar has dissolved add the strawberries, cook for approximately 15 minutes, with the lid on until the strawberries are totally soft.*

🍴 *Remove the vanilla pod and lemon. Blend/blitz the mixture.*

🍴 *Soak and prepare, as above the gelatine. Add to the puree, mix until dissolved.*

🍴 *Pass the mix through a coarse sieve. When cooled totally, pour some onto each of the cooled and set panacottas, and allow to set in the fridge.*

Vanilla Cheese Cake *Colette swears by this* | **Císte Cáise Fanaile**

BASE:

- Biscuits (Digestive or ginger nut)
- 75g of butter (at least)

- Digestive or ginger nut biscuits (in terms of the amount, it's a bit of trial and error to judge how thick you want your base).

- Crush the biscuits by hand to work out your frustrations or in a blender.

- Melt the butter in a pot.

- Add the crushed biscuits to the melted butter and mix well.

- Spread the mixture into a spring loaded cake tin.

- Place in the fridge and allow it to set firmly.

CHEESE CAKE MIX:

- 200g Cream cheese
- 6 tablespoons Icing sugar
- Juice of lemon
- 600mls Double cream
- 1 Vanilla pod deseeded

- Beat together cream cheese, icing sugar and vanilla seeds until smooth.

- Add the lemon juice.

- Lightly whip the double cream into soft peaks in a separate bowl.

- Fold the whipped cream into the cream cheese mix. Make sure not to whip it. You want it to be light and airy.

- Put the folded mixture into the cake tin and smooth out the top.

- Let it set in the fridge.

When ready EAT!

Sweet Mince | Sólas Milis

🍴 *Cook the sliced apples until they are soft.*

🍴 *Stir to a smooth pulp. Leave to cool.*

🍴 *Once cooled stir in all the other ingredients – mix it well.*

🍴 *Place in a sterilised airtight jar/container until ready to use – this will keep for months.*

I usually make a full sized sweet mince pie, using the flaky pastry recipe.

- 1lb Cooking apples; peeled and cored.
- 12ozs Raisins
- 6ozs Sultanas
- 6ozs Currants (depending on your likes you can replace this with extra raisins/sultanas
- 6ozs (Atora) suet.
- 7ozs Soft brown sugar.
- Zest & juice of 1 lemon (zest finely grated/chopped)
- $1/2$ teaspoon mixed spice
- 3 tablespoons of brandy – Macieira arís!

Photo by Ladyheart at Morguefile.com

Rice Pudding | Maróg Ríse

- 2 ozs Pudding rice
- 1 Pint of milk
- 1oz sugar (try vanilla sugar)
- Some ground nutmeg

🍴 *Grease an ovenproof dish.*

🍴 *Add the sugar, rice and milk.*

🍴 *Give it a stir to make sure it's all mixed.*

🍴 *Sprinkle a little nutmeg over the top.*

🍴 *Cover and place in the oven. It's easier to put it on a baking tray – less risk of spillage!*

🍴 *Bake for 2 hours.*

This mix serves 4. For more just double the ingredients.

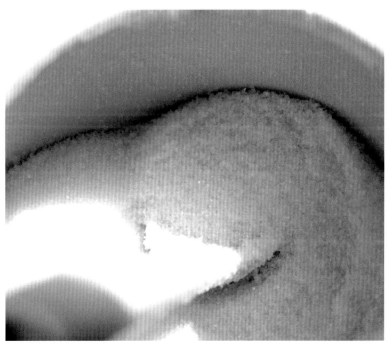

Photo by Alvimann at Morguefile.com

POSTSCRIPT | IARNÓTA

As well as Ted and Pádraic's recipes I have included an offering from Sinn Féin Leas Úachtaran Michelle O'Neill and North Belfast MLA and former minister Carál Ní Cuílín.

But that's only because they ordered me to. They freely admit it is because they want associated with Ted and Pádraic's recipes.

There is also a Lemon Drizzle yoke from Iseult Lanigan. It is here because it is scrumptious. Iseult sent me this caca milis to Stormont with her mammy, Mary Lou. I shared it with the team in Room 316 before sampling it myself. Then I sleekitly and speedily took the remainder of it back home with me to finish off all on my own. Go raibh maith agat Iseult.

Finally Maura Dougan, a much younger sister of Gerry Kelly, is a wizard at boiled fruit cake. Our good friend Rita O'Hare goes into gastromanical raptures at even a hint of a morsel of Maura's cake.

Once on the train from New York to Washington Rita became quite emotional as we shared a few slices of Maura's finest fare.

"It reminds me of my mother's baking" Rita sobbed through a mouth full of raisins and currants, cherries and moist cake.

"The sweet scent of the fruit, the fragrance of the tea, the taste……..." she whimpered before, like me and Iseult's Lemon Drizzle, stealing it away in her handbag for secret herself alone consumption later.

I must confess our Negotiating Team never got sight of Maura's cake, to my knowledge. It never survived that long. So it is here for you with thanks to Maura and in honour of Rita.

Photo by mariask at Morguefile.com

Chomh maith leis na hoidis a sholáthair Ted agus Pádraic, tá curtha ar fáil agam thíos moladh ó Leas-Uachtarán Shinn Féin Michelle O'Neill agus ceann eile ón Chomhalta ar Bhéal Feirste Thuaidh, agus iar-Aire, Carál Ní Chuilín.

Ach an t-aon chúis leis sin gur thug siad orm sin a dhéanamh. Admhaíonn siad go hoscailte go bhfuil siad ag iarraidh iad féin a cheangal le saothar Ted agus Pádraic.

Tá Lemon Drizzle ann fosta a bhuí le hIseult Lanigan. Tá sé anseo nó tá sé blasta. Chuir Iseult an cáca milis seo chugam lena Mamaí, Mary Lou. Roinn mé leis an fhoireann i Seomra 316 sular thriail mé féin é. Ansin, thug mé go glic is go gasta é chun an bhaile, lena chríochnú liom féin. Go raibh maith agat Iseult.

Agus i ndeireadh na dála, Maura Dougan. Deirfiúr de chuid Gerry Kelly, agus í i bhfad níos óige. Draoi leis na cístí torthaí bruite atá inti. Bíonn an t-aoibhneas ag sileadh lenár ndlúthchara Rita O'Hare má luaitear, fiú amháin, gurbh fhéidir go mbeidh giota de chíste Maura ar fáil.

Tráth dá raibh, ar an traein ó Nua Eabhrac go Washington, tháinig tocht ar Rita mar a d'ith muid cúpla slisne den chíste le chéile.

"Bheir sé bácáil mo mháthar i mo cheann," ar Rita ag snagaireacht agus a béal lán de rísíní is cuiríní, de shilíní agus den chíste bhog.

"Dea-bholadh milis na dtorthaí, cumhra an tae, an blas…" ar sise de ghuth caointeach sular ghoid sí, mo dhála féin leis an Lemon Drizzle ó Iseult, sular ghoid sí an rud ar fad chuici féin, curtha sa mhála láimhe lena chaitheamh i modh rúnda ar ball.

Caithfidh mé a admháil nach bhfuair an Fhoireann Idirbheartaíochta deis ar chíste Maura riamh, go bhfios dom. Níor mhair sé chomh fada sin. Mar sin de, tá sé ar fáil duit anseo a bhuí le Maura agus in ómós do Rita.

Banana Bread | Arán Banana

But first to an Bhean Uasal Ní Chuilín. Carál's recipe is for Banana Bread.

Ach ar dtús báire, an Bhean Uasal Ní Chuilín. Oideas Charál don arán banana.

Pre-heat the oven to 180c or gas mark 4

Mix all the wet ingredients with the bananas. Sieve flour and bicarb in gradually until smooth. Pour into a greased 2lb tin and bake for about an hour.

- 10oz plain flour
- 1 teaspoon of bicarb of soda
- 4oz butter
- 8oz castor sugar
- 2 eggs
- 4 ripe banana mashed
- 1-2 teaspoons of vanilla extract
- Half teaspoon mixed spice
- A handful of sultanas
- A squirt of honey

Photo by thelesleyshow at Morguefile.com

Portuguese Upside Down Pineapple Cake |
Císte Bunoscionn Portaingéalach Anainn

- 200g Sugar
- Seven or eight pineapple slices

- 5 eggs
- 150g of sugar
- 100g 0f self raising flour

- Custard

This recipe comes from Michelle O'Neill. I can't vouch for it because I've never ate it. I have enjoyed fish prepared by Michelle in Room 316 but for reasons known only to herself she refused my many requests for that fine dish. Instead she sent me a Roast Garlic and Chorizo Soup yoke but Ted disputed the authenticity of this soup as a Clonoe speciality so I give you Tyrone's favourite pudding.

Is le Michelle O'Neill an ceann seo. Ní thig liom é a dhearbhú nó níl blaiseadh de ite agam. Tá béile éisc a d'ullmhaigh Michelle ite agam i Seomra 316 ach ar chúiseanna nach bhfuil a fhios agam, dhiúltaigh sí go leor iarratas uaim an béile galánta sin a dhéanamh arís. Ina áit sin, chuir sí sú ina raibh Gairleog Rósta agus Chorizo. Cheistigh Ted ionracas an ruda seo maidir le hoidhreacht Thír Eoghain. Mar sin féin, molaim daoibh an mharóg is ansa le muintir Thír Eoghain.

FOR THE CARAMELISED PINEAPPLES:

🍴 *Lay your pineapple slices on the bottom of an appropriate cake tin, preferably ring tin*

🍴 *Caramelise sugar in sauce pan over moderate heat. Pour over pineapple Rings*

🍴 *Mix the eggs and sugar and flour in an electric mixer until smooth.*

🍴 *Pour over the caramelised pineapple and put in pre heated oven at 180 for 35 - 40 minutes.*

Eat hot or cold and if you like it, with custard.

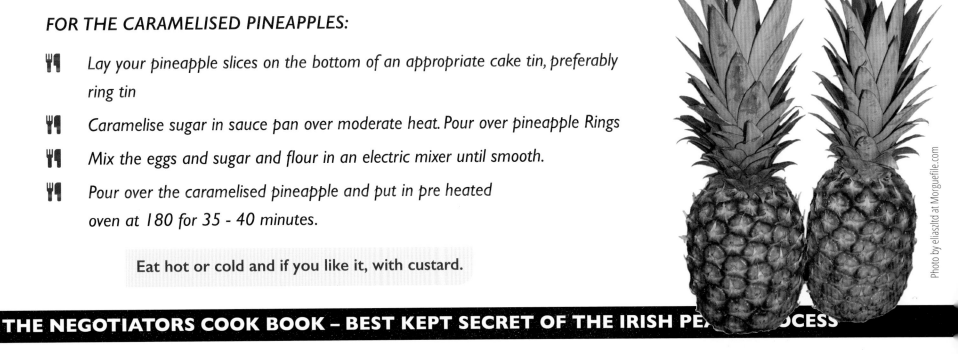

Photo by eliaszltd at Morguefile.com

Iseult's Lemon Drizzle Cake | Císte Steall Líomóide le Iseult

Just to test us older citizens Iseult instructions are metric. But don't let that put you off. Persist and you will be delighted with yourself. A sugar hit par excellance.

Heat oven to 180c. Fan 160c. Gas 4

🍴 *Cream 225g unsalted butter and 225g castor sugar together until pale and fluffy*

🍴 *In a separate bowl whisk eggs with a fork. Add all eggs little by little while whisking continuously.*

🍴 *Sift in the flour slowly, making sure not to curdle mixture.*

🍴 *Grease a cake tin (8x4) and line it with grease proof paper.*

🍴 *Put the misture in tin and bake for 45-50 minutes*

FOR THE DRIZZLE:

🍴 *Mix the 90g castor sugar with the juice of the 2 lemons*

🍴 *Once the cake has cooled pour the liquid over it.*

FOR THE ICING:

🍴 *Whisk (Iseult recommends an electric yoke) icing sugar, unsalted butter, lemon juice and lemon zest together in a large bowl.*

🍴 *Beat in milk and increase whisk speed until light and fluffy.*

🍴 *Plaster cake with icing.*

Eat.

- 225g unsalted softened butter
- 225g castor sugar
- 4 medium eggs
- Zest of 1 lemon finely grated
- 225g self raising flour.

For the drizzle;
- Juice 2 lemons
- 90 g castor sugar.

Icing;
- 250 g icing sugar
- 60 g unsalted softened butter
- 20 ml fresh lemon juice
- 1 teaspoon lemon zest
- 4 teaspoons whole milk.

And finally **Maura Dougan's Boiled Fruit Cake**
Císte Torthaí bruite le Maura Dougan

This makes two cakes.

- *Put first lot of ingredients into a pot and bring slowly to the boil, simmer for a minute.*

- *Leave to cool.*

- *Beat up 4 large eggs, sieve in 8 ozs plain flour and 8 ozs self raising flour.*

- *Add to cooled mixture, splash in some brandy or sherry and a wee sip of orange juice plus a handful of Walnut and glace cherry pieces.*

- *Pre heat oven at 180. Divide mixture between two loaf tins lined with paper.*

- *Bake in middle of oven for 1 hour to 1 hour 10 minutes.*

- 750g dried mixed fruit.
- 8 ozs butter
- 12 ozs granulated sugar
- 16 fluid ozs water
- 4 heaped teaspoons mixed spice
- 2 level teaspoons Bicarbonate of Soda

- 4 large eggs
- 8 ozs plain flour
- 8 ozs self raising flour

- Brandy or sherry
- Walnut
- Glace cherries

Photo by MaxStraeten at Morguefile.com

THE NEGOTIATORS COOK BOOK – BEST KEPT SECRET OF THE IRISH PEACE PROCESS

THE NEGOTIATORS COOK BOOK – BEST KEPT SECRET OF THE IRISH PEACE PROCESS

• **ROOM 316 DINERS CLUB:** Michelle O'Neill, Seán Mag Uidhir, Mary Lou McDonald, Conor Murphy, Pádraic Wilson, Carál Ní Cuílín, Gerry Kelly, Declan Kearney, Ted Howell and Stephen McGlade

• Gerry Adams, Martin McGuinness and Ted Howell